AIR WAR

Antony Loveless

 Crabtree Publishing Company

www.crabtreebooks.com

Crabtree Publishing Company

www.crabtreebooks.com   1-800-387-7650

Copyright © **2009 CRABTREE PUBLISHING COMPANY**.
All rights reserved. No part of this publication may be reproduced,
stored in a retrieval system or be transmitted in any form or by
any means, electronic, mechanical, photocopying, recording, or
otherwise, without the prior written permission of Crabtree
Publishing Company.

**Published
in Canada
Crabtree Publishing**
616 Welland Ave.
St. Catharines, ON
L2M 5V6

**Published in the
United States
Crabtree Publishing**
PMB16A
350 Fifth Ave., Suite 3308
New York, NY 10118

Content development by Shakespeare Squared
www.ShakespeareSquared.com
First published in Great Britain in 2008 by ticktock Media Ltd,
2 Orchard Business Centre, North Farm Road,
Tunbridge Wells, Kent, TN2 3XF
Copyright © ticktock Entertainment Ltd 2008

Author: Antony Loveless
Project editor: Ruth Owen
Project designer: Sara Greasley
Photo research: Lizzie Knowles
Proofreaders: Robert Walker,
    Crystal Sikkens
Production coordinator:
    Katherine Kantor
Prepress technician:
    Katherine Kantor

With thanks to series
editors Honor Head
and Jean Coppendale.

Thank you to Lorraine
Petersen and the
members of nasen

Picture credits:

Corbis: Aaron Allmon II/U.S. Air Force/Reuters: p. 4–5;
    Aero Graphics, Inc.: cover; Kyle Niemi/U.S. Coast
    Guard/ZUMA: p. 10; Katrina V. Walter/U.S. Navy/
    Reuters: p. 13 (top)
Crown Copyright: Antony Loveless: p. 1, 2, 6, 7, 8–9, 9 (top),
    12–⌐ᵒottom), 14, 15, 16–17, 18, 19, 20–21, 22, 23,
    2⌐   29 (top), 31
G⌐   ⌐: p. 11 (bottom); AFP: p. 5 (bottom), 11 (top),
            ⌐om)
    ⌐ock: p. 24, 25

   ⌐ effort has been made to trace copyright holders, and we apologize in
   ⌐ance for any omissions. We would be pleased to insert the appropriate
   ⌐cknowledgments in any subsequent edition of this publication.

Library and Archives Canada Cataloguing in Publi⌐

Loveless, Antony
    Air war / Antony Loveless.

(Crabtree contact)
Includes index.
ISBN 978-0-7787-3812-1 (bound).–ISBN 978-0-7787-3834-3 (pbk.)

    1. Air warfare--Juvenile literature. 2. United States. Air
Force--Juvenile literature. 3. Air forces--Juvenile literature.
I. Title. II. Series.

UG631.L69 2008   j358.4'14   C2008-905956-5

Library of Congress Cataloging-in-Publication Data

Loveless, Antony.
    Air war / Antony Loveless.
        p. cm. -- (Crabtree contact)
    Includes index.
    ISBN-13: 978-0-7787-3834-3 (pbk. : alk. paper)
    ISBN-10: 0-7787-3834-5 (pbk. : alk. paper)
    ISBN-13: 978-0-7787-3812-1 (library binding : alk. paper)
    ISBN-10: 0-7787-3812-4 (library binding : alk. paper)
    1. Air warfare--Juvenile literature. 2. United States. Air Force--
Juvenile literature. I. Title. II. Series.

UG631.L588 2008
358.4'14--dc22
                                      2008039394

Contents

CHAPTER 1

AIR FORCES AT WORK

During a war, soldiers on the ground need protection. They need protection from enemy planes. This is the job of the air force.

The air force shoots down enemy planes. Sometimes, it bombs enemy planes on the ground before they can take off.

F15E Strike Eagle

Air-to-air missile

The Royal Air Force (RAF) has 1,000 aircraft. The United States Air Force (USAF) has over 6,000 aircraft.

When not at war, the air force's job is to stop air attacks on **civilians**.

An attack could come from enemy aircraft or from terrorists.

Air forces also help people affected by **natural disasters** such as floods and earthquakes.

*May 2008 - Supplies are loaded on a USAF plane for **victims** of a **cyclone** in Myanmar.*

CHAPTER 2

QUICK REACTION ALERT

One important area of work for the RAF is "Quick Reaction Alert" or QRA. If a plane is **hijacked** or something unusual happens, fighter plane crews are ready to react.

Controller

Every minute of every day, there are thousands of aircraft flying in United Kingdom (UK) **airspace**.

At an RAF base, controllers watch the signals sent from aircraft. The controllers also watch for enemy planes flying into UK airspace. If the controllers see something unusual, the fighter plane crews are told to "stand by." This is QRA.

As the pilots run to their planes, **ground crews** prepare the planes for quick a take-off.

Pilot

In an emergency, every second counts!

"Our day lasts for 24 hours. We do one day on, one day off. We live in our flying gear. We sleep fully kitted up. It saves time if we have to **scramble**."

QRA *pilot*

Within minutes of the QRA, the jets are in the air. The fighter planes can **accelerate** at up to 1,535 miles per hour (2,470 km/h). This is twice the speed of sound.

Typhoon F2s

"Nothing compares to the feeling when you climb into the sky in a fast jet on a dark, miserable rainy day and break through cloud into the blue sky and bright sunlight. It's the best office view in the world!"

Fighter Pilot Sam Cowan

CHAPTER 3

EMERGENCY HELP

The USAF and RAF do not just fight wars and terrorists. They also help around the world when there is a major emergency.

In 2005, the city of New Orleans was flooded during Hurricane Katrina.

Here, a CH47 Chinook drops giant bags of sand into the flooded area. The sandbags act as a barrier to help hold back the flood water.

The USAF rescued people who were trapped in the flooded city.

In 2004, a 30-foot (9 meter) high wave called a tsunami, hit the coastline of many countries in Southeast Asia.

The USAF and RAF were on the scene within hours.

Air force planes delivered food and medical supplies to people affected by the tsunami. They also delivered heavy digging equipment. This equipment was needed to clear large objects such as fallen trees and bricks from houses destroyed by the tsunami.

Air force men and women also helped on the ground. They looked after people who were hurt during the tsunami. They cleared blocked roads and helped rebuild homes.

A C17 transport plane loaded with supplies to help the tsunami victims

CHAPTER 4

THE PILOTS

What is it like to be one of the men or women who fly fighter planes for the RAF or USAF?

When not at war, fighter pilots perform QRA duty. They also fly training missions called "sorties." A sortie may last from two to four hours. These training missions often include low-level flying and pretend air-to-air battles. A pilot's normal day also includes **intelligence**, weather, and weapons **briefings**.

A pilot performing pre-flight checks before a sortie

"Every time we get airborne, we do something to make us better pilots. There is always a point to the sortie."
Fighter Pilot Sam Cowan

Helmet with protective clear and tinted visors

Calf leather flying gloves

One-piece flight suit

Map pocket

Inflatable G-pants

15

"Everyone who flies fighter jets feels lucky. When you walk to your aircraft, it's awesome. You might think I haven't been **supersonic** for a while, so you will do that. Having that power at your fingertips is just amazing."

Fighter Pilot Sam Cowan

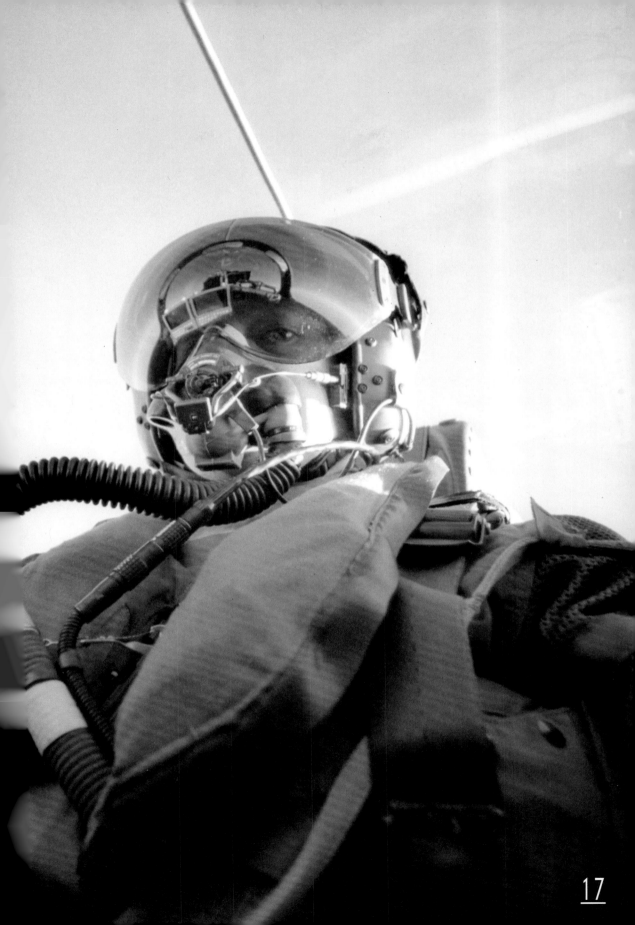

*Pulling a tight turn
at low-level*

18

Unlike airline pilots, air force pilots are trained to fly at low levels.

This is so they can fly planes under enemy **radar**. Low-level flying is fast and very dangerous. It needs to be practiced regularly.

All the flying is done by the pilot. There is no help from computers.

The pilot is flying at 7 miles per minute (11 kilometers per minute). The plane is just 151 feet (46 meters) off the ground.

The smallest mistake could mean certain death for the pilot!

Low-level Tornado F3s

Pilots must learn to cope with g-force.

G-force is the force pushing against an object when moving at high speeds. G-force is what you feel when you ride down a roller coaster.

Pilots experience greater g-force the faster they fly. As g-force gets higher, it affects the pilot's body. Blood is dragged to the pilot's legs and feet. This could kill the pilot. Special pants called g-pants help to stop this.

Next, a pilot may lose his or her peripheral vision. This means the pilot cannot see out of the corners of his or her eyes. It is like looking through two narrow tubes.

Finally, everything turns black and white. The pilot may even pass out.

As g-force gets lower, the pilot's senses return to normal.

Dual tinted and clear visors
to protect the pilot's eyes

Microphone
on/off switch

OFF

ON

The breathing regulator supplies
a pilot with oxygen. High up,
the air is too thin to breathe.

Oxygen hose

CHAPTER 5

THE AIRCRAFT

TYPHOON F2

The RAF's newest aircraft is the Typhoon F2.
It is the most advanced fighter jet in the world.

Each plane costs over 100 million dollars!

The F2 can climb nearly one
mile (1.6 kilometers) into the sky
within 30 seconds of take-off.

It can **cruise** at supersonic speeds.

In air-to-air combat, a fighter pilot must keep his or her eyes on the fight at all times.

Visor

The F2 has a sight-activated missile-firing system. This system allows the pilot to fire missiles at a target just by looking at the target!

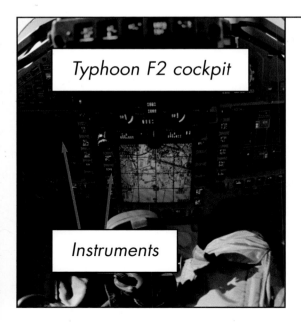

Typhoon F2 cockpit

Instruments

The F2 computer sends information about fuel and **altitude** onto the pilot's visor. This means the pilot does not have to look down to check the cockpit instruments.

F-22 RAPTOR

The F-22 Raptor is an American fighter jet. It is used to attack enemy targets on the ground and in the air.

The F-22 is armed with six air-to-air missiles

The F-22 uses **stealth technology**. This means it is very hard for enemy radar to detect the plane. It gives the F-22 time to attack before the enemy spot it on their radar.

The F-22's top speed is over
1,550 mph (2,494 km/h).

Fighter jets need to be light and fast. This means they can only carry enough fuel for 60 to 90 minutes of flying. Most sorties last longer than this.

A **Combat Air Patrol** (CAP) can last for hours. During a CAP, fighter jets patrol an area looking for enemy aircraft. Air-to-air refuelling allows the fighter jets to stay in the air for longer periods of time.

Large planes called tankers deliver fuel to other planes.

Fighter jets waiting for fuel and those that have been refuelled protect the tanker plane.

Tanker plane

Hose

Basket

Fuel is delivered using a basket-like piece of equipment on the end of a long hose.

XB

Jet taking on fuel

The USAF and RAF use a lot of different support aircraft during wars and rescue missions.

Chinook CH47
helicopter

The Chinook CH47 is a twin-engine, heavy-lift helicopter. Its main job is moving troops and supplies to battlefields.

The Chinook has a wide loading ramp at the back.
Supplies can be dropped from the ramp.

Ramp

The Hercules C-130 is used to transport troops and
equipment. It is also used to rescue people from
dangerous areas.

Hercules C-130

The Hercules can do short take-offs and
landings using very rough runways.

NEED-TO-KNOW WORDS

accelerate The rate at which a plane increases its speed

airspace The air (sky) above a country in which aircraft can fly. Each country controls its airspace and says which aircraft can fly there

altitude The height of an aircraft above the ground

briefing Giving accurate information to the pilots about a situation

civilian A person who is not in the air force, army, or navy

cyclone A storm with very powerful winds

co-ordination Being able to make your body and senses work well together. For example, when a pilot's eyes see danger, the pilot's hands must react quickly to fire on the enemy

cruise To fly for a length of time at one speed

ground crew The non-flying members of an air force. They take care of the aircraft

hijack To take over and control an aircraft by force

intelligence Information about the enemy. It is usually secret

natural disaster A disaster caused by nature

radar A method of detecting distant objects. Radar can find an object's position and speed by sending radio waves that reflect off the object's surfaces

scramble Quickly entering an aircraft and flying somewhere in response to an alert

stealth technology Technology that makes an aircraft almost invisible to radar

supersonic A speed that is greater than Mach 1 (the speed of sound). Mach 1 is about 770 mph (1,239 km/h)

victim A person who is hurt, killed, or affected badly by an event

PILOT TRAINING

Becoming a trainee

To be given a place as a trainee pilot, you must have excellent exam results. You must also be fit with good eyesight. Pilots also need above average **co-ordination** skills.

This is the pilot's view in a Hawk aircraft simulator.

Training

Pilots train on full-motion flight simulators. The simulators handle and respond exactly the same as real aircraft. However, the trainee pilots do not have to leave the ground.

Non-flying jobs

Most air force jobs are on the ground. There are hundreds of non-flying jobs that keep each pilot and aircraft in the air. These jobs include air traffic controllers, mechanics, cooks, medics, and drivers.

AIR FORCES ONLINE

http://science.howstuffworks.com/military-aircraft-channel.htm
A close-up look at different military aircraft

www.usaf.com/intro.htm
Learn about the history of the USAF

www.goang.com/games/
Different games related to military aircraft

http://www.f22fighter.com/
Everything you need to know about the F-22 Raptor

Publisher's note to educators and parents:
Our editors have carefully reviewed these websites to ensure that they are suitable for children. Many websites change frequently, however, and we cannot guarantee that a site's future contents will continue to meet our high standards of quality and educational value. Be advised that children should be closely supervised whenever they access the Internet.

INDEX

Printed in the U.S.A. - BG